THE ILLUSTRATED
MOTORCYCLE LEGENDS

ROY BACON

SUNBURST BOOKS

Acknowledgements

The author and publishers wish to acknowledge their debt to all who loaned material and photographs for this book. Most came from the ever helpful press office at BMW (GB) Ltd. and from the photo archive staff at the head office of BMW in Munich, both of whom responded to my lists to search out my needs. Other pictures which helped to complete the story came from *Motor Cycle News* courtesy of editor Rob Munro-Hall and EMAP whose archives hold the old *Motor Cycle Weekly* files. Old friend Don Mitchell kindly loaned material from his extensive stock to fill in some gaps. Thanks to all who helped.

Published 1994 by Sunburst Books, Deacon House, 65 Old Church Street, London SW3 5BS.

ISBN 1 85778 039 6

Designed by Anthony Cohen

Printed and bound in China

CONTENTS

AN AIRCRAFT START

BMW - purveyors of a single model type for some 60 years before introducing a new design, and that to be contrary to those offered by their competitors. One of the few firms left to still build motorcycles and cars, the two living happily together. A firm who set special standards and produced riders' motorcycles, machines better suited for the long ride rather than a quick blast up the road. Staid in keeping to one design, still there after 70 years, but avant-garde in so many ways and often leading the industry down new paths.

The firm has its roots in aircraft engines and from this came the quartered blue-and-white badge, representing a whirling propeller shimmering against a blue sky and first seen in 1917. That year Bayerische Motoren Werke GmbH, or BMW, became the outcome of mergers but the Armistice stopped the aircraft work so it had to turn to other fields.

The first 1917 BMW badge from which the modern blue and white quartered one comes.

Below: A BMW engine powered this aircraft to a world altitude record in 1919 when they were banned from flying.

BOXER TWINS

· ·

One new field was motorcycles, but early efforts proved crude, so their brilliant Max Friz set to work and conceived the model R32, first shown in Paris in 1923. That machine set out the essence of the BMW which continues to this day. The 494cc engine was of the boxer or flat-twin type, but having the cylinders set across the frame, not in line. The three-speed gearbox bolted to the back of the engine to give unit construction and drove the rear wheel by shaft.

The engine and transmission was brilliant in concept, even if none toopowerful, but the frame and forks were less so, front suspension being by trailing links. At first braking was by a dummy belt rim at the rear only, but a front drum brake was soon added.

The R32 was soon involved in German races, winning the 1924 national title, and was joined by two new models in 1925. One was the R37, a racing version of the R32 having overhead valves, the other the 247cc R39 single. This began a 40-year practice of offering a single which copied the twin layout but with the cylinder vertical. The R39 had overhead valves, these being fully enclosed on both single and twin engines, an alloy cylinder head and the barrel cast in one with the crankcase, a pressed-in liner providing the running surface; very advanced for the year. It also had a drum brake added at the front end of the drive shaft, just aft of the gearbox, a feature to be used by BMW for some years and an improvement on the dummy belt rim.

The touring R42 was added for 1926, the engine developed from the R32. It had the drive shaft drum brake and provision for a sidecar, alternative axle ratios being listed, another practice to continue down through the years. It was joined by the ohv, 494cc R47 in 1927, the R32 and R37 being dropped.

The range was revised for 1928, the R39 going to leave just twins for a few years. While the R42 and R47 ran on for their final year, four new models joined them, although all six retained the original style which was now looking somewhat dated. The new four comprised the R52 of 486cc, its engine a long-stroke side-valve unit, and the ohv R57 which kept the original square dimensions and 494cc capacity. The two were matched by a larger pair, the 745cc R62 which had side valves and the long stroke of the R52, and the 736cc ohv R63 which kept the old 68mm stroke of the R32 and R57.

Early BMW flat-twin engine installed in a Victoria. Max Friz soon improved on the whole concept.

Above: The brilliant R32 which launched the BMW range in 1923. The concept of a flat-twin engine driving back to the gearbox and thence by shaft to a rear bevel box continues to today.

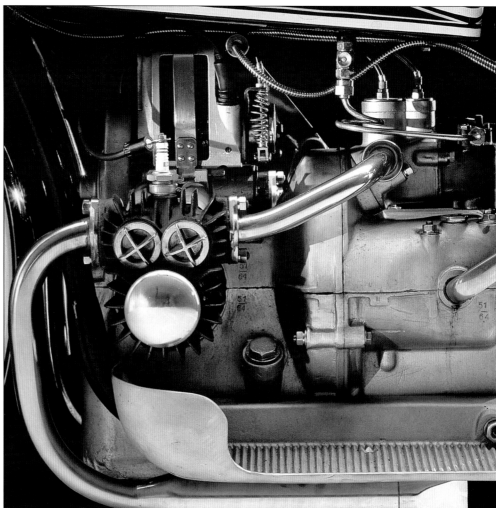

Right: The 494cc engine and gearbox unit of the R32, so simple, compact and logical for its job.

Left: The same simple, sturdy construction applied to other aspects of the R32, including the frame, seat and controls.

Below: Franz Biber raced the new BMW to success in 1924 and is seen here at Solitude.

For racing, BMW produced the R37 in 1925, the engine having overhead valves but based on the R32.

The first BMW single was the 1925 247cc R39 which had ohv as did all that followed. Otherwise much as the twins.

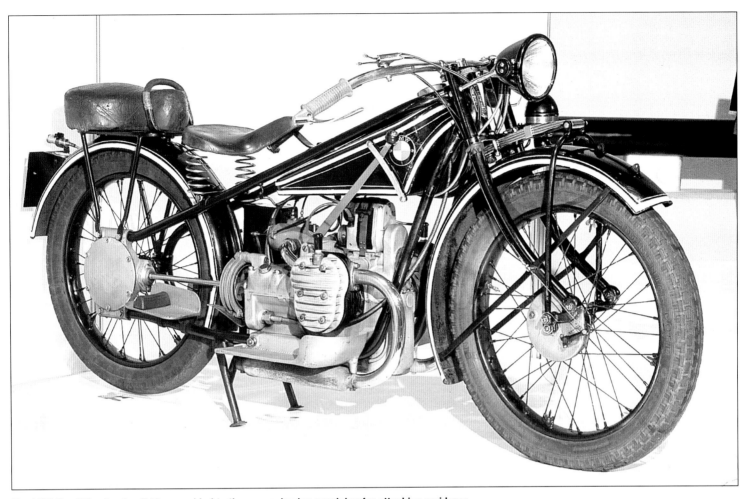

For 1926 the 494cc touring R42 was added to the range, having provision for attaching a sidecar.

The R47 of 1927 replaced the R37, having an improved 494cc engine.

One of the four new models for 1928 was the 486cc R52 with side valves.

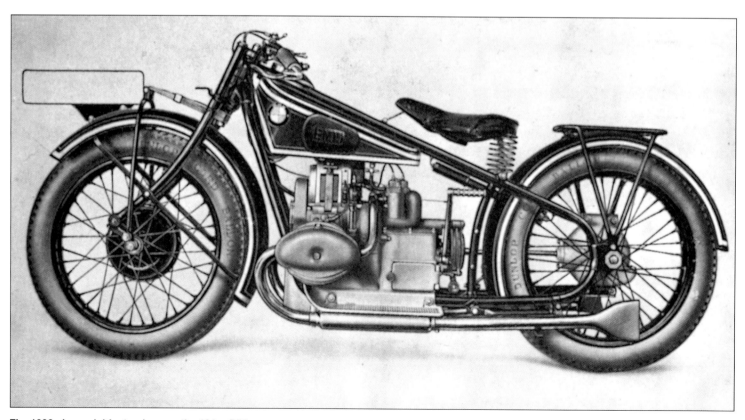

The 1928 ohv model for touring was the 494cc R57.

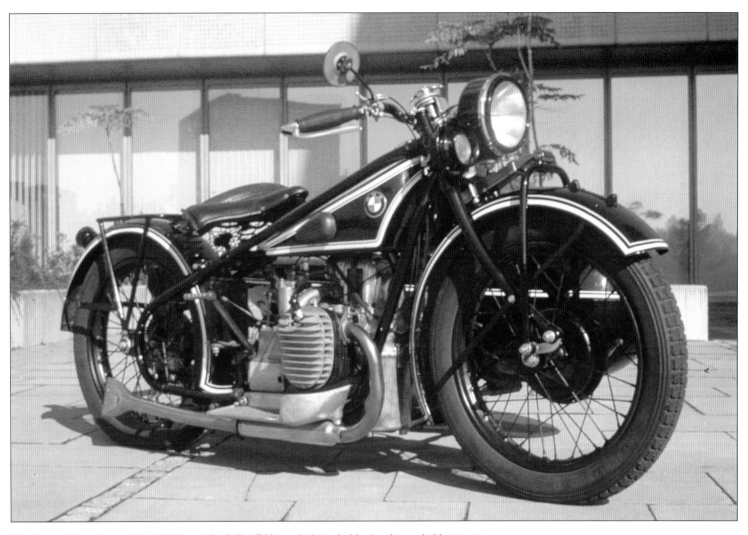

The larger side-valve model of 1928 was the 745cc R62, again intended for touring and sidecar use.

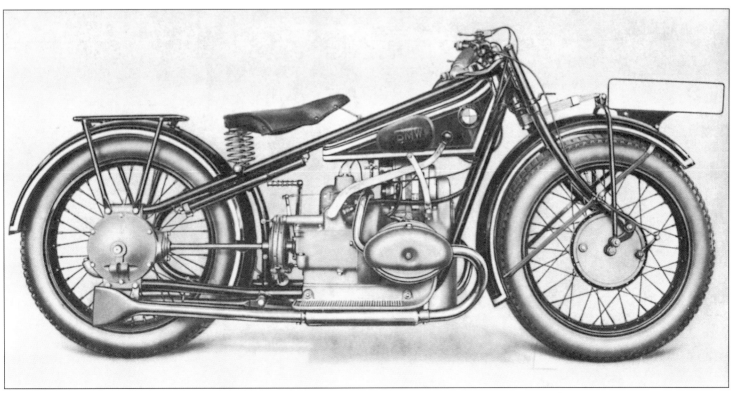

The faster overhead-valve model was the 736cc R63 of 1928 which used the same frame and forks as the smaller models.

PRESSED STEEL

· ·

T wo more models appeared in 1929, both using existing engines in a new style of frame and fork. Although the concept and outline remained, construction was by pressed steel in place of tubing, this being lined out in a manner which accentuated the Teutonic image. It was a European theme, found mainly in Germany, and in contrast to the saddle tank style being adopted in Britain. The models themselves were the R11 with the 745cc side-valve engine, and the R16 which used the 736cc ohv unit.

It was 1929 when BMW entered the record breaking field, using their 750cc twin fitted with a supercharger. It was crudely streamlined but, ridden by Ernst Henne, it set a new world figure at 216.05km/h, the first time a German machine held the record. Henne was to take the record several more times during the 1930s, also the sidecar one in 1931.

By the end of 1930 the road range was down to the R11 and R16 in their pressed-steel frames, but they were joined by a new single, the 199cc ohv R2. This too had the frame and forks made from pressed steel but differed in having a drum brake incorporated with the bevel box. It was joined by a second single in 1932, the 401cc ohv R4, this being fitted with a four-speed gearbox from 1933. As with the twins, the larger single was offered with solo or sidecar axle ratio, and they ran on to 1936 and 1937.

A new pressed-steel frame appeared for 1929 on the 745cc R11, the front forks taking the same style, while remaining the trailing links of the past.

The overhead valve version of the new style was the R16 which used the 736cc engine.

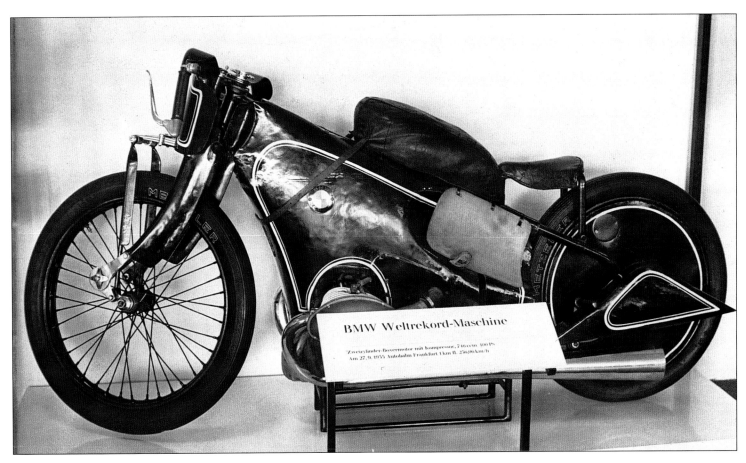

One of the record breakers ridden by Ernst Henne to set new maximum speed figures. This is the 750cc machine In its 1935 supercharged form.

The single came back in 1931 as the 199cc R2 in a pressed-steel frame.

Larger single-cylinder model was the 401cc ohv R4.

Last of the older generation of racing machines, this supercharged solo ran at the Nürburgring in 1933.

TELESCOPICS
••••••••••••••••••••••••••

I n 1935 BMW took their front suspension from ancient to modern in one move to introduce the first telescopic front forks with hydraulic damping, basically as still used by nearly all modern machines. The new forks were only used on twins at first, these being the 745cc side-valve R12 and 736cc ohv R17, both fitted with four-speed gearboxes. The machine style remained much as before, the frames still pressed steel and the fork lining as on the trailing links.

A year later, in 1936, BMW moved both ways. The major change was to add the R5, this having a tubular frame and the 494cc ohv engine plus the telescopic forks in a slimmer style. Only the bevel box mounting reflected the old, the rest was new and in a style able to live for years. The other move was to offer the 305cc, ohv R3 single with pressed-steel frame and trailing-link forks, but only for the one year.

In 1936 the 500cc engine, plus a supercharger, was used by Henne to again set the world speed record, the machine and rider now fully enclosed. He returned in 1937 and moved the figure on to 279.503 km/h where it was to stay until 1951. At the same time the factory returned to road racing, running the 500cc blown twin, and recruited Jock West from Britain to ride for them in 1937 when he won the Ulster

Grand Prlx. For 1938 they added Georg Meier who became European champion that year and won the Senior TT the next. During this period BMW were involved in the International Six Days Trial, the ISDT, as part of the German team.

The R3 was replaced in 1937 by the 192cc R20 and 342cc R35, both having telescopic forks, the first a tubular frame and three speeds, the second keeping to the pressed steel frame, but with the four speeds of the R3. Also new that year was the R6 which used the R5 cycle parts to house a 600cc side-valve engine.

Four new twins were introduced for 1938, all having the addition of plunger rear suspension to give them a style which continued on to 1954. The models were the 494cc ohv R51, 597cc ohv R66 and two side-valve machines, the 600cc R61 and 745cc R71. From the past the R12 and the two singles continued and were joined by the 247cc ohv R23, an enlarged version of the R20 which was dropped that year.

First appearance of the BMW telescopic fork was in German racing in 1934. Here, Joe Craig and Jimmy Guthrie of Norton weigh up the new design.

The new forks were used in the ISDT late in 1934, this being one of the 750s and featured on the front of the 1936 catalogue.

Side-valve model fitted with the new forks was this 745cc R12 which retained the pressed-steel frame and its white lining.

Above: The overhead-valve machine was the 736cc R17, the forks moving from ancient to modern in one jump.

Right: During 1935, BMW introduced a new, supercharged, 500cc engine fitted into a tubular frame for racing events, it making its debut at Avus in June.

Opposite page: The new engine and frame were used in the 1935 ISDT, this one ridden by Ernst Henne.

For 1936, the 494cc R5 appeared in the tubular frame, its style to remain modern for many years.

Below: The 1936 305cc R3 used the old frame and forks so was only listed for one year.

In striking contrast to the old record breaker, Henne turned to this streamlined machine using the supercharged 500cc engine to set new records in 1937.

The works 500cc, supercharged racing BMW as campaigned successfully in the late 1930s, it having the telescopic front forks and plunger rear suspension.

Georg Meier winning the 1939 Senior TT in the Isle of Man, a famous victory.

The works twin as used in the 1937 ISDT, kitted out to suit the event and its demands.

The first single in the tubular frame was the 1937 192cc R20 whose forks lacked hydraulic damping.

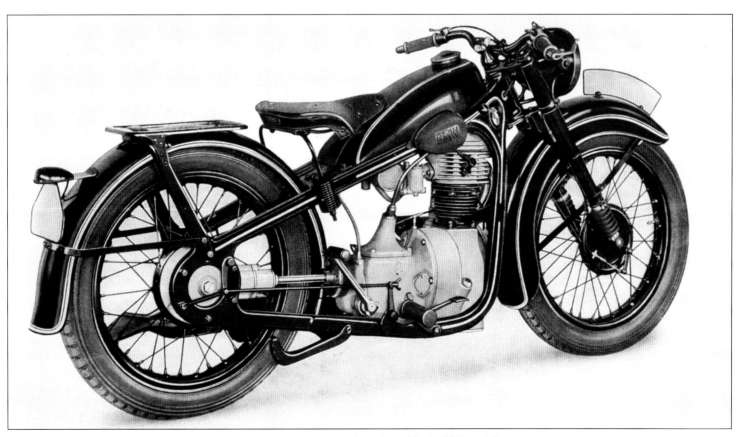

Older in style was the 1937 342cc R35 single, but it did have a four-speed gearbox, this the 1939 model.

Cover from the 1938 brochure showing vast use of BMW machines by the Wehrmacht.

Another new model for 1937 was the 600cc R6 which used a side-valve engine but was only listed for one year.

The 1938 brochure played on the shaft drive and plunger rear suspension of the models.

One of four new 1938 models, all having plunger rear suspension, was the 494cc R51.

The larger 1938 ohv twin was the 597cc R66, its style to run for years.

Smaller of the 1938 side-valve models was the 600cc R61.

For sidecar use there was the 745cc R71, largest of the 1938 models.

The 1938 single was the 247cc R23, it having ohv, telescopic forks but no rear suspension.

Georg Meier at Quarter Bridge during his 1939 Senior TT ride.

WEHRMACHT

The existing range ran on to 1940 or so, but the R12 stayed on a little longer as a military machine. It served the needs of the Wehrmacht well enough, along with service versions of the R35 and R4 singles, but during the war was joined by the R75, a machine developed for cross country work with a sidecar.

The R75 was a massive outfit intended to cope with mud or snow equally well while carrying heavy loads of men and materials. To this end, it used the 745cc ohv engine coupled to the four-speed gearbox. This incorporated both a two-speed gear to give four high or low ratios and a reverse gear. More gears went in the rear bevel box which included a drive across to the sidecar wheel, a differential to split the power between the driven wheels, and a means to lock this for use when off-road.

All the mechanics were housed in a massive duplex frame fitted with telescopic forks. The wheels had heavy-duty spokes and interchanged, a spare being carried on the sidecar tail, and all were braked. It scaled 420kg unladen, much more when fuelled and armed, served on many fronts, but was superseded by the Kubelwagen for it took skill to get the best from it.

Military version of the R12, a machine which did sterling service until the more complex R75 came along.

Service version of the R35 which retained the pressed-steel frame but had telescopic forks.

The service R4 kept both the pressed-steel frame and old-style, trailing-link front forks.

Massive, complex and with gears for fast, slow, reverse and the sidecar wheel as required - the wartime 745cc R75.

The R75 came with a sidecar which could carry men, fuel, arms and ammunition as well as a spare wheel.

Restored R75 sidecar with one choice of fitment, a heavy calibre machine gun.

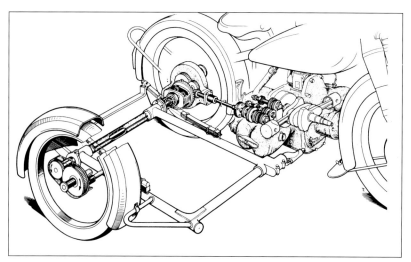

Above left: Power transmission from engine/gearbox assembly to rear wheel differential via a driveshaft.
Above right: Differential on cardan housing of rear wheel used for the first time in motorcycle building for sidecar drive.

POSTWAR CHANGES

A t the end of the war much of BMW was in ruins, but a nucleus of the workforce remained at one plant. For a while they made things in aluminium, the one raw material they had. Pots, building fittings, even a bicycle kept them going until they could return to motorcycles. First they built a prototype of 125cc, the R10, which was a two-stroke but still a flat twin having shaft drive.

Finally, in March 1948, the first postwar model was shown at Geneva. It was the R24, much as the R23, but with the engine improved and driving a four-speed gearbox. Production began at the end of the year for 1949, the single being joined by a twin for 1950. This was the R51/2, little altered from its pre-war form, and during the year the single became the R25 with plunger rear suspension. For 1951 it had minor changes as the R25/2 while the twin became the R51/3 with a much revised engine, the camshaft drive being gear driven rather than by chain. It was joined by the R67, this having a 594cc ohv engine to offer a little extra power.

During the early postwar period Germany was banned from international events so Meier campaigned the old blown twin from 1947 to 1950 with much success. After that, the ban was lifted, the blower removed and Walter Zeller joined the team to take over from Meier. A revised solo racer appeared and some well known riders including Geoff Duke and John Surtees rode the flat twin but without any real success. On three wheels, in sidecar racing, it was totally different although it took a little while for this to materialise.

The sports R68 made its debut in the range at the Geneva show early in 1952, offering more power from its 594cc engine and a twin-leading-shoe front brake to stop it. This completed the range which ran little altered until 1955 when a new frame and forks were introduced; the R25 continuing for one last season, the R67 in /3 form also remaining up to 1956 as a sidecar machine.

By then the firm had made its mark road racing on three wheels, starting in 1954 when Wilhelm Noll won the world title. From then to 1974 the firm would dominate the class, only the URS created by Helmut Fath troubling them. Fath had already taken one title using a BMW, but it was Max Deubel with four and Klaus Enders with

Below: Early postwar prototype 125cc R10, a two-stroke engine but still having shaft drive.

Opposite: Production line of the R24 as in 1949.

six who were the most successful. Over the 20 years, a BMW won 112 of the 128 classic races, a record unlikely to ever be equalled anywhere.

Back with the road range, 1955 brought new models in the form of the 494cc R50 and 594cc R69 twins plus the 247cc R26 single. All had a new frame with rear suspension not unlike lengthy plungers but in fact, of the pivoted fork type. At the front the telescopic forks gave way to the long leading link type known as the 'Earles fork'.

Further publicity came from more record breaking carried out in 1954 and 1955, this time mainly over long distances and times but including the 10km sidecar at 212.7km/h. The firm was part of Germany's ISDT teams in the early 1950s, but this was to fade, although not to stop.

The road range added the 594cc R60 for 1956, this being as the existing twins but intended as a sidecar-hauling model to replace the R67 which went at the end of the year. This left four machines in the range and they all ran on to 1959 and a major crisis for BMW, the company.

250 c.c. The Motorcycle of Quality

The first postwar model was the R24 single, prewar frame but a better engine.

First postwar twin was the R51/2, much as prewar.

The single gained plunger rear suspension for 1950 to become the R25.

For 1951 the twin had its engine revised to create the R51/3.

BMW

R 67

The 594cc R67 joined the R51 In 1951, running on as a sidecar machine as seen here in its 1955 form.

As raced in 1950 in Germany, a R75 bored out to 900cc, minus supercharger and fitted with twin carburettors.

Works BMW as ridden by Walter Zeller during 1953.

Production racing RS54 as used by a number of riders of that era.

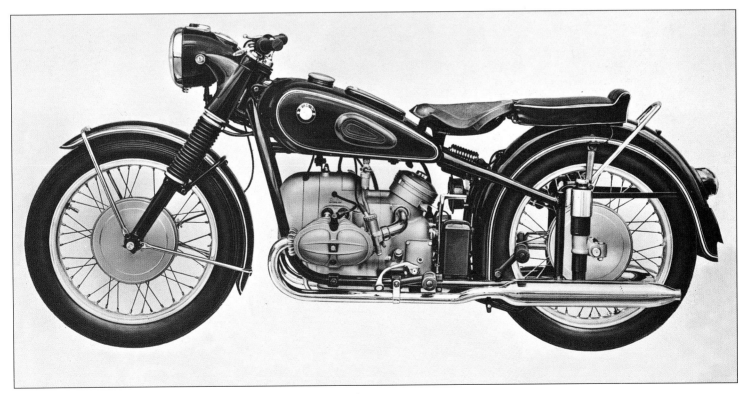

The sports 594cc R68 made its debut in 1952 to offer a 100mph potential.

From 1953 the single became the R25/3 with a new frame and forks plus engine improvements.

Wilhelm Noll won BMW's first sidecar world title in 1954 to start a two-decade run of domination.

Many BMWs were used in sidecar racing and here Alwin Ritter ties his false leg in place at Blandford in 1960.

Below: Much developed outfit of Florian Camathias, one of the fastest of the BMW pilots.

Klaus Enders won six world titles using BMW-powered outfits and is seen here during the 1966 TT.

Below: For 1955 there was a new frame, new Earles forks and three models, this the 494cc R50.

BMW

R 69

the fastest German production motorcycle

Freie Fah
OPEN DRIVE

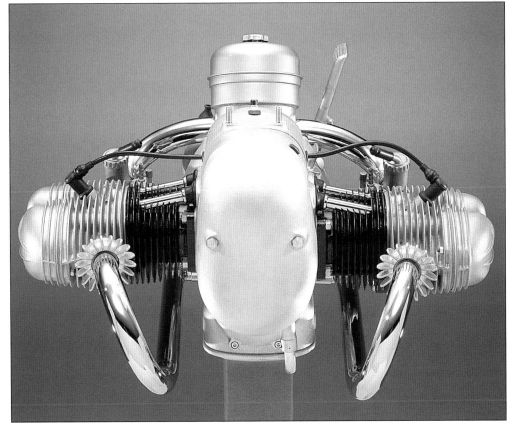

Above: The 1955 594cc R69, the larger of the two twins and fitted with a diaphragm clutch.

Left: This is the R69 engine unit, the R50 being virtually identical.

An R26 as built from 1955 to 1960 but in the optional white as seen in 1993.

Wilhelm Noll breaking sidecar records in 1955 using full streamlining.

Left: Walter Zeller in 1955 on the solo, setting new 10-km and 10-mile records.

Below: An R25 which ran in the 1951 ISDT.

The R68 as prepared for the ISDT of 1952.

New for 1956 was the 594cc R60 and, intended for sidecar use, it found favour with police and military riders.

CRISIS
•••••••••••

The BMW crisis had its beginnings in the early to mid 1950s as production, the German economic miracle, began to outstrip demand. This shifted demand from two wheels to four and BMW were caught out with their products. Both their motorcycles, and the cars they had been building for many years, were good but too expensive for most people's budget. The resulting drop in sales was inevitable.

An interim measure was the Isetta, a bubble-car powered by an R25 engine, it having four wheels, but with the rear pair close enough to be classed as a three-wheeler for tax and insurance. It sold well and was later stretched to add rear seats. Next came the 700, a small car, but one that kept to a flat-twin, motorcycle engine.

By 1959, the lack of a new middle-class car was dragging the firm down but a crucial and historic meeting saved the day and enabled BMW to continue until the new car, the 1500, was launched in 1961. From it stemmed the modern series while the motorcycles ran on to be revitalised in the years to come.

This was far from an immediate event, the two-wheelers running through the 1960s with very little change right up to 1969. In 1960 the revisions introduced the R27, R50S and R69S, the first a further edition of the 247cc single having the engine unit rubber mounted. The other two models were sports versions of the touring twins, both of which continued with small changes.

The pattern was set for the 1960s. In a shrinking market, BMW offered what they had always produced, an expensive, refined machine which sat ill at ease amongst the café racers of the decade. BMW buyers were mainly experienced riders who

The Isetta bubble car which used the R25 engine and proved very popular until the Mini came along.

enjoyed the way the Munich twin could cover 500 miles and leave them fresh. Few machines were its equal at this form of fast, long-distance travel.

This image was helped by some production racing between 1959 and 1961, when they won the prestigious events at Barcelona, Thruxton, Silverstone and the Bol d'Or. This success was capped by their taking the world 24-hour record in 1961 at 109.24mph. It emphasised both the speed and the endurance of the flat twins.

The range shrunk over the years. First to go was the R50S after 1963, for sports buyers preferred the larger model. Then the R27, now extremely expensive for a 250, and the R60, now too slow, went after 1967 to leave the R50 and R69S. That year, those supplied to the USA had telescopic forks fitted in place of the Earles type, these having been developed for the ISDT machines.

Finally, during 1969, the old had to make way for the new so BMW gave the Friz concept another twist - they moved the camshaft.

Right: A motorcycle flat-twin engine powered the 700 coupé which bridged the gap to the next car range.

Below: The front of the 1961 brochure which played upon the firm's record breaking successes.

MOTORCYCLES

Rubber mounts were used for the engine and gearbox unit of the R27 to reduce the effects of vibration.

Sports version of the smaller twin was the R50S, hard to distinguish from the tourer.

Al Knapp rode a BMW in the 1959 Daytona 200 and here heads two others into the North Turn on the combined beach and road circuit.

Flat out at Silverstone in one of many production machine races in which BMWs did so well.

The larger sports twin was the R69S, a fast machine enjoyed by those discerning riders who could afford its high cost.

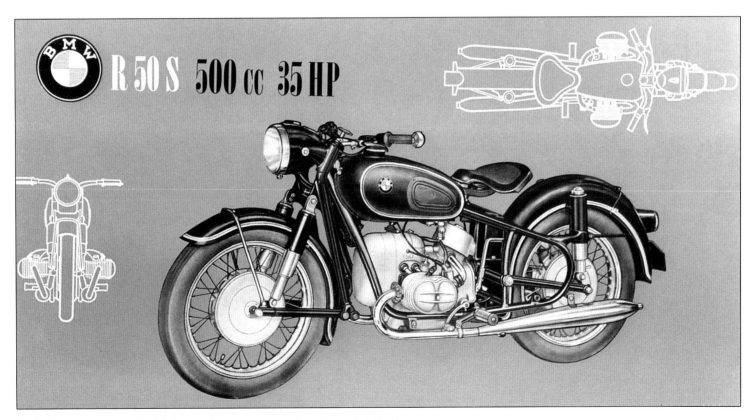

First of the old to go was the R50S, small sports models seldom being too popular.

Next was the R27, too expensive and coming under attack from the new breed of small sports models from Japan.

Below: A touring twin seen in 1993, now more appreciated for its abilities than then.

The R50 soldiered on to the end of the decade, selling to a decreasing market.

Last of the old line was the R69S which remained fast, quiet and reliable to the end.

Many BMWs hauled a sidecar, this extensively modified one indicating the lengths that owners would go to for extra fuel capacity, weather protection and luggage facilities.

NEW TWIST

•••••••••••••••••••

T he new range, introduced in 1969, was a fresh approach to the flat twin and comprised three models, the 498cc R50/5, the 599cc R60/5 and the 746cc R75/5. All had a great deal in common and kept true to the BMW concept of unit construction and shaft drive. There was a new and lighter frame, long-travel telescopic front forks, 12-volt electrics and an electric starter as standard for the two larger machines.

Inside the engine the old pressed-up crankshaft was replaced by a forged one, the stroke being common to all, a high-pressure lubrication system was introduced and the camshaft went under the crankshaft where it was driven by chain. On the outside the crankcase carried covers enclosing both the air filter and the starter motor mounted on the top.

Behind the engine went a diaphragm clutch which drove a four-speed gearbox and this the rear wheel. The assembly went into a duplex frame having pivoted-fork rear suspension while both wheels had full-width alloy hubs, straight spokes and alloy rims. The front brake had twin-leading shoes, the rear was rod operated. A massive 22-litre fuel tank gave the machines range and the whole aspect was shorter and more compact than in the past.

Reaction among conservative BMW owners was mixed, as expected, and this was accentuated by the use of colour. Traditionally, BMWs were finished in black with white lining, or the reverse of this - usually for the police. Suddenly, BMWs, well the R50 and R75, were in silver grey and lined in blue for the tank and mudguards, just the R60 keeping to the black of old.

Smaller petrol tanks having chrome-plated side panels came for 1972 along with small side covers to hide the battery and more colour choices. The larger tank remained an option, preferred by many, and during 1973 the rear fork was length-

Smallest of the new range of twins was the 498cc R50/5, here fitted with high bars.

ened to improve the handling. That year, BMW ran two R75/5 machines round the TT circuit for a week and were awarded the Maudes Trophy for this demonstration of reliability

The range was modified for 1974 to become the /6 series, much as before but having the headlamp and instruments revised to a more modern style. At the same time a five-speed gearbox appeared, the R50 was dropped and the R60/6 and R75/6 were joined by two R90 models. Both had an 898cc engine, achieved by increasing the bore further, and the /6 was much as the others although both it and the R75/6 had a single front disc brake, an option for the R60/6.

The second new big twin was the R90/S, a sports machine fitted as standard with a cockpit fairing and twin front discs. It featured a large, graceful fuel tank, and a stylish finish in a silver which gradually changed to a smoked grey in an effective way. And it was quick for the times.

In the middle came the 599cc R60/5, only the ignition key stuck out of the headlamp a feature from the past.

Top of the new range was the 746cc R75/5, all three machines virtually identical.

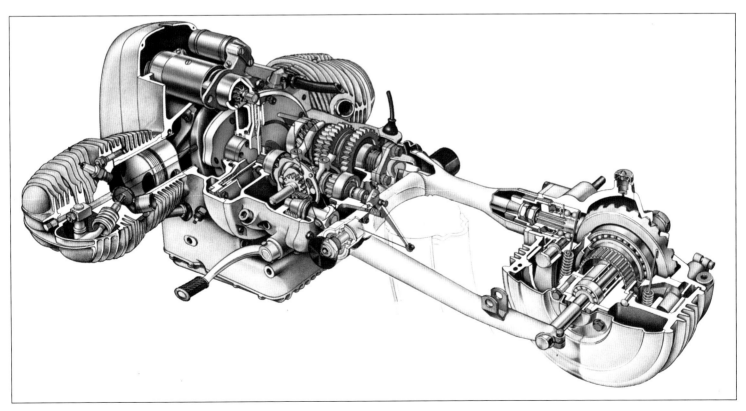

Engine, gearbox, shaft drive, rear suspension and rear wheel introduced for the 1969 /5 models.

Right: The two R75/5 machines which ran round the TT circuit for seven days under appalling weather conditions, a feat that gained BMW the prestigious Maudes Trophy.

Below: For 1974 the /6 range took over, this being the R60/6, now the smallest of the twins.

The R75/6 became the middle twin for 1974, featuring a disc front brake.

Largest of the 1974 twins had 898cc engines, this the R90/6 which mirrored the two smaller models.

BMW broke new ground with the R90S of 1974, offering this sports model with a cockpit fairing and a stylish paint scheme.

Right: Oblique view of front wheel having twin perforated brake discs.

FAIRINGS AND OFF-ROAD

I t was detail changes up to 1976 when the two R90 models were replaced by three larger ones, and the smaller twins became /7 types. The new twins were opened up even further to 980cc to become the R100/7 and R100S with cockpit fairing. The third new model was the Rl00RS which broke new ground by being sold complete with an integral fairing, another BMW first. It was based on the R100 and BMW managed to achieve a fairing shape that worked at high speed while having a form that looked stylish. It proved a winner, very popular with owners and enabled the serious rider to maintain high speeds for some 200 miles if need be.

Late in 1977 the R75/7 was replaced by the 797cc R80/7 and for 1978 there were two new, entry-level models, the 473cc R45 and 650cc R65 . These were very similar and shared many parts with the larger models but were styled to differ, the frame being more compact and cast-alloy wheels being fitted.

At the end of 1978 the R60/7 was dropped, its place taken by the R65, while the R100/7 became the Rl00T. A new model, the Rl00RT, was much as the Rl00RS, but had a larger touring fairing. This set the range for a year, but 1981 brought new

In 1976 the twins became /7 models, this the R60/7 and the smallest.

Factory line of the R75/7 model in Berlin, a
far cry from the early postwar conditions.

models, one for a field fresh to BMW. This was the trail market for which the R80G/S
was evolved, the R80/7 being dropped.

BMW's off-road involvement had, up to then, been as factory machines in the ISDT
where they performed with distinction. The new model reflected this but was based
firmly on the road R80, except for its rear suspension. This was a true swinging arm
– or monolever as BMW termed it – having one arm and spring unit on the right.
Other changes were to suit the use and reduce weight so there was a two-into-one
exhaust, high-level silencer, 21 inch front wheel and no rev-counter.

The R80G/S was in at the start of a new trend towards trail bikes that were limited
in their off-road use but performed well on the road. It proved popular, sold well
and brought a cry for a version having road tyres. The capability of the works
machines was emphasised by Hubert Auriol winning the 1981 Paris to Dakar rally, a
feat he repeated in 1983 with Gaston Rahier winning for the next two years.

Meanwhile, for 1981, the Rl00T became the R100 and the Rl00S the Rl00CS, while
the Rl00RT was fitted with a Nivomat self-levelling rear-suspension unit to offer a

constant ride height. A useful option was heated handlebar grips which were most welcome in winter, while the BMW range of motorcycle clothing extended to a safety helmet. As with their machines, it differed from the rest in having the chin bar section able to hinge up.

The R65LS was added for 1982, this being a styling exercise which added a cockpit fairing and other details to the R65, while the mid-year brought two more R80 models in response to customer demand. The basic machine was the R80ST which used the monolever rear end, the other the R80RT, a smaller version of the 1-litre tourer complete with its big fairing. The range ran on as it was for 1983 for BMW were busy on a totally new project.

For 60 years BMW had kept to the concept of the flat-twin engine, unit gearbox and shaft drive. Their market niche was the select and discerning one, never inexpensive but one in which they were very successful. However, the performance envelope of the 1980s had moved on and BMW had to move with it, but – and this was the truly hard part – without losing their special image and style.

Engine capacity went up to 980cc in 1976 to create the R100/7 as the basic model.

One of the advertisements for the R100RS which moved the concept of the sports machine a good step forward.

Above left: Many police forces used the R100RS, which is why cars move over for them, but these are R100/7 models fitted with the RS fairing.

Above: The sports model with cockpit fairing became the R100S, seen here from above.

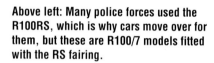

Left: Selection of detail points of the BMW range of 1976.

Before 1978 the mid-range twin was enlarged to become the R80/7.

The new entry-level BMW for 1978 was this 473cc R45, similar to the existing models but styled to differ.

Larger entry model was the 650cc R65 which used the same cycle parts as the R45.

For 1979 the base model large twin became the R100T, often fitted with panniers for touring.

Above: The R100RT was introduced for
1979 as the major touring machine, fitted
as standard with a larger fairing than the
RS model.

Right: Factory GS80 used in the late 1970s
from which the off-road models were
derived.

The off-road R80G/S which appeared in 1981 and proved a fine machine on the road up to around 90mph.

The true swinging-arm rear suspension of the R80G/S.

Right: Hubert Auriol riding in the Paris-Dakar rally; he won the event twice, as did Gaston Rahier, both riding BMW.

Below: Basic large twin for 1981 became the R100, a quick and capable model.

The R100S became the R100CS for 1981 but kept to the format established by the R90S.

Even the BMW helmet differed from those made by other firms, both visor and chin bar hinging up to aid removal.

A 1982 styling exercise produced the R65L/S which featured a cockpit fairing.

In response to demand, BMW used their off-road model as the basis for the R80ST for 1982, a light and handy mid-range motorcycle.

For the tourer who did not require a one-litre engine, BMW added the R80RT which retained the large fairing.

The Futuro was a concept model shown at the Cologne show in 1980 but not taken any further.

K SERIES – THE BRICKS

he result was the K series, launched late in 1983 as the basic K100, the K100RS with sports fairing, and a little later, the K100RT tourer. Essentially one design with minor variations, all had a 987cc four-cylinder, watercooled engine equipped with twin overhead camshafts and fuel injection. Unlike any of their opposition, the in-line four lay along the machine, just right to drive the five-speed gearbox, and on its side so the crankshaft went on the right and the cylinder heads to the left, just right for the shaft to drive the rear wheel.

The engine hung from a tubular frame, suspension was by telescopic front and monolever rear, while the wheels were cast alloy and fitted with disc brakes. The overall result worked well, giving ample performance, but the front end was deemed light at speed and the brakes somewhat wooden. The style led to it being called the 'brick'. The RS worked better, being faster and more stable at high speed.

The advent of the K-series resulted in all the R100 models being dropped early in 1984, a decision which did not meet with universal approval. For 1985 the K models continued while the R80ST became the R80, the R80RT changed to the monolever rear suspension and a Paris-Dakar version of the R80G/S joined the stock one. It differed in having a massive fuel tank, special seat, rack and crash bars. At the end of the year the R45 and R65LS were dropped, while the R65 changed to the monolever frame.

For 1986 the K-series was extended to add two models fitted with three-cylinder 740cc engines, these being the K75C with cockpit fairing and the K75S which had the sports fairing. They were joined by the basic K75 for 1987, along with special editions of the K75S and K100RS, these having styling changes in the main. Also new was the K100LT, a luxury version of the K100RT, but the remaining addition to the range was the return of an old friend, the R100RS twin. Demand was such that BMW just had to bring it back.

The K-range continued for 1988, when anti-lock brakes (ABS) became a factory option for the K100 models, but without the special K75S, while the off-road twin range was replaced. The 650cc engine was used to create the R65GS, and the other models were the R80GS and Rl00GS, both of which had a new swinging arm. This was patented as the BMW Paralever and, unlike the monolever, was jointed and linked to keep the rear wheel under better control. Another clever detail was the design of the wire-spoked wheels which allowed the use of tubeless tyres.

A second old friend returned for 1988 in the shape of the R100RT but at the end of the year both the R65 and R65GS left the general market, although remaining on the German one with a restricted output engine. The K75C and K100RT went but there were two new models for 1989. One, a Paris-Dakar version of the R100GS followed the lines of the earlier R80G/S type, but was not sold in the UK.

The second new model for 1989, the K1, was a super-sports version of the K100 which moved BMW further forward. The engine was revised to four-valve heads, there were many detail improvements, the Paralever rear suspension was fitted, and the finish and graphics were bright and eye catching in red or blue with yellow – a step to match the opposition even if it raised eyebrows among traditional BMW owners. The result was striking but acceptable.

Most of the range continued as it was for 1990, the ABS option available for the K75, but the standard and special versions of the K100RS were replaced by a single model fitted with the 16-valve K1 engine and Paralever rear end. New in selected markets was the K75RT, the triple in touring guise, while the parts special to the Paris-Dakar model became available as a kit for either GS model.

The R65GS was dropped for 1991 along with the K100 which had not been sold in the UK in 1990. The rest continued with moves to control exhaust emissions using a catalytic converter on the 16-valve fours, and simpler systems for the rest. A Limited Edition version of the K100LT was new, while the K75RT became generally available.

Above: Launched late in 1983, the BMW K-series comprised three models, the basic K100, the sports K100RS and the touring K100RT as lined up here.

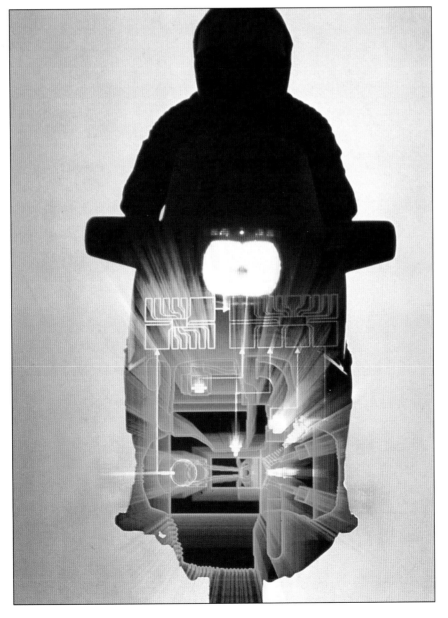

Left: Taken from the launch brochure, this striking graphic indicates the basis of the K100 design.

Right: The unusual K100 engine, gearbox and rear drive assembly, the engine laid on its side.

Below: Base model K100 fitted with optional luggage rack and mudflap.

Sports K100RS, fast and stable at high speed.

The touring K100RT, this one fitted with options for carrying luggage.

Right: Wind tunnel testing the new model for air flow around the mirrors.

Below: From 1985 the base twin became the R80, this a police model, seen in Tenerife in 1993.

The R80RT changed to monolever rear suspension for 1985.

A Paris-Dakar version of the R80G/S joined the standard version for 1985, fitted with a larger tank and other special items.

The R65 in its 1985 form with the monolever rear suspension.

A K100 on show in 1985, little altered from its launch.

First of the triples was the K75C which was fitted with a cockpit fairing mounted to the handlebars.

In contrast the K75S had its fairing and headlamp fixed directly to the frame.

Above: The base K75 joined the other triples for 1987 this being a later model.

Right: Special edition of the K75S fitted with engine spoiler and custom paint and colour finish.

The luxury tourer K100LT was added for 1987 supplied fully equipped with many extras.

The R100RS returned to the range for 1987 brought back by popular demand for this classic twin.

Above: Hard braking in the wet became
easier on a K100 model in 1988 thanks to
the option of ABS.

Right: Close up of the installation of the
ABS pressure modulator and the rear
wheel sensor monitoring the toothed gear.

The Paralever rear suspension arm appeared in 1988 for the off-road models, this being the R80GS.

The R100GS fitted the new Paralever rear end and the wire wheels common to the off-road models.

A Paris-Dakar version of the R100GS appeared for 1989, on the lines of the earlier type.

Back came the RI00RT in 1988, another model the public refused to do without.

Above: Super-sports motorcycling came to BMW in 1989 in the form of the K1, a 16-valve engine hidden beneath the special panels which blended into the front mudguard.

Left: Cut-away drawing of the K1 showing some of the internal detail.

Later K100RS of 1990 which used the 16-valve K1-engine and the Paralever rear end, this a 1992 model.

New for some markets in 1990 was the K75RT which went on general release the next year.

Kit of Paris-Dakar items available for either GS model.

NEW CONCEPTS

BMW moved their range in two directions for 1992, adding a retro model to meet the trend for the classic look, and replacing the K100LT models by an enlarged, 1093cc, K1100LT machine. It used the 16-valve engine and had all the refinements. The retro Rl00R went the other way, being based on the Rl00GS with Paralever and wire wheels, but styled by using the round valve covers from the old R68.

The manner in which BMW kept ahead was demonstrated even more vividly in 1993. The Rl00R was joined by the smaller R80R while the K-series had the sports four replaced by the larger K1100RS, neither unexpected. The real news was a major revamp for the boxer engine and a radically new form of front suspension to go with it.

The new machine, the R1100RS, retained the air-cooled flat-twin engine, but this was much revised to include four-valve heads, each with a single camshaft. The capacity went up to 1085cc, the engine oil assisted the cooling, fuel injection was used and a catalytic converter fitted. If the engine was a major step forward, the front suspension was even more so. What looked conventional at a glance, was innovative, having the telescopic forks attached to the frame by a wishbone and upper ball joint. A single, remote, spring unit controlled fork and wheel movement, the system being known as Telelever.

BMW showed their forward thinking in 1992 with a concept drawing of a motorcycle for the future. A little later they built the C1, an idea which blended elements from car, motorcycle and scooter. At the same time they developed a trail model

New for 1992 was the K1100LT which fitted an enlarged 16-valve engine and the Paralever rear end; lots of options in addition to the standard luxury.

totally at odds with their history. For the first time a BMW had chain final drive, this dictated by the use of a 652cc single-cylinder Rotax engine, the complete machine being built by Aprilia in Italy. Listed as the F650 Funduro, it was seen as an entry level model able to run well both on and off the road. It was one of the new models for 1994.

Also new for 1994 was the R1100GS, a monster trail model which used the new boxer engine, the Telelever front suspension and Paralever rear end to create a machine for long-distance touring, able to go off-road, and having style. The engine was detuned, suspension travel increased and a massive fuel tank fitted to suit this purpose. Other new models for 1994 were the R100R Mystik, a restyle of the retro model, and a Special Edition K1100LT which came even better equipped for the serious tourer.

It all showed how BMW kept ahead while remembering their past. The single, the new boxer, the old twins, the K-series, the new and radical suspension systems, all indicated the tradition and innovation behind the blue-and-white quartered badge.

For the retro market there came the R100R Roadster combining the old valve covers with the new Paralever.

By using the enlarged engine, BMW created the K1100RS for 1993.

Above Two major steps in the boxer story, an RIOORS on the left of an RIIOORS, both showing how BMW move ahead of the field.

Right: The new front end which used a lower wishbone and top ball-joint to carry the telescopic forks, all controlled by a single unit.

Left: Far from the BMW image was the F650 trail model of 1994 which used a single-cylinder engine from Italy and, shock - horror, chain final drive.

Below: The R1100GS of 1994 was a monster trail model which incorporated the latest BMW developments in engine and suspension.

A Special Edition K1100LT was listed for 1994, offering everything the serious tourer could desire.

An owner's concept: a K-series custom seen in 1993. Few were brave enough to attempt such work.

Left: The BMW image: 4,000 rpm, accelerating from a bend, the stereo on the music channel and the journey nearing its end. Long but not tiring.

Below: Family tree: R32, R100R and R1100RS - a boxer remains a boxer.

BMW MODELS

Singles

200cc	R2, R20
250cc	R39, R23, R24, R25, R26, R27
300cc	R3
350cc	R35
400cc	R4
650cc	F650

Twins

side valve

500cc	R32, R42, R52
600cc	R6, R61
750cc	R62, Rll, R12, R71

overhead valve

450cc	R45
500cc	R37, R47, R57, R5, R51, R50, R50S, R50/5
600cc	R66, R67, R68, R69, R60, R69S, R60/5, R60/6, R60/7
650cc	R65, R65LS, R65GS
750cc	R63, R16, R17, R75, R75/5, R75/6, R75/7
800cc	R80/7, R80G/S, R80RT, R80ST, R80, R80GS, R80R
900cc	R90/6, R90/S
1000cc	R100/7, RI00S, RI00RS, R100SRS, R100T, RI00RT, R100, RI00CS, RI00GS, RI00R
1100cc	R1100RS, R1100GS

Triples

750cc	K75C, K75S, K75, K75S special, K75RT

Fours

1000cc	K100, K100RS, K100RT, K100LT, K100RS special, K1, K100LT-LE
1100cc	K1100LT, K1100RS